T0274385

What's in this book

This book belongs to

_____

艾文很忙! Ivan is busy!

学习内容 Contents

沟通 Communication

说说闲暇活动
Talk about leisure activities

背景介绍:
艾文的暑假生活多姿多彩,每天都有不同的活动。

生词 New words

★	时间	time
★	功夫	kung fu
★	唱歌	to sing
★	跳舞	to dance
★	上网	to go online
★	运动	to do sports
★	再	again, once more
	照片	photo
	游泳	to swim
	舒服	well
	游戏	game
	生病	to get sick
	疼	to ache

句式 Sentence patterns

我要运动，运动，再运动。
I will keep doing sports.

跨学科学习 Project

了解京剧，设计京剧脸谱
Learn about Beijing Opera and design a facial make-up pattern

文化 Cultures

中国功夫
Chinese kung fu

参考答案：
1 I listen to music/play with my friends.
2 It is playing basketball/dancing.
3 Yes, he is.

Get ready

1 What do you do in your spare time?

2 What is your favourite leisure activity?

3 Ivan plays badminton and dances and sings with his friends during the holidays. Is he busy?

shí jiān
时间

武 尚

故事大意：
暑假里，艾文参加了各种各样的活动，而伊森则天天在家上网打游戏，最终生病了。伊森决定要向艾文学习，多运动，过健康生活。

gōng fu
功夫

"功夫"通常指中式搏斗形式。英文kung fu一词是由中文"功夫"音译过去的。

放假了，艾文很忙，时间不够用。
星期一，他学中国功夫。

参考问题和答案：
What is Ivan doing? (He is learning Chinese kungfu.)

星期二，他学唱歌和跳舞。老师还给他拍了照片。

参考问题和答案：
1 What is Ivan going to do? (He is going swimming.)
2 How does Ethan look? (He does not look well. He looks ill.)

星期三，他想叫伊森一起去游泳，但是伊森不舒服。

参考问题和答案：

1 What is wrong with Ethan? (He is ill and is having a headache.)
2 Why do you think he is ill? (Because he played too many online games.)
3 What do you think Mum is telling Ethan? ('You shouldn't play online games every day.')

伊森因为天天上网打游戏，所以生病了，头疼。

参考问题和答案：
What advice does Ivan give Ethan? (He suggests that Ethan do more exercise.)

yùn dòng
运动

"你应该多运动，像我一样，就没时间生病了。"艾文说。

参考问题和答案：

1　What has Ethan made? (He has made an exercise plan.)

2　Is Ethan going to do sports again and again in the same day? (Yes, he is.)

上午　下午　晚上

zài

再

"再"表示重复或又
一次做某件事情。

"好，我不再打游戏了。我要运动，运动，再运动！"伊森说。

Let's think

1 Recall the story. What did Ethan and Ivan do? Match them to the activities.

2 What is the best way to spend the holidays? Discuss with your friend and draw below.

New words

1 Learn the new words.

延伸活动：
老师描述图中人物／动物（见下方参考表达），学生根据描述猜猜老师
讲的是哪些人／动物，并在图中写数字，对人／动物进行排序。

2 Listen to your teacher and point to the correct words above.

听听说说 Listen and say

🎧 03 **1** Listen carefully. Number the pictures.

🎧 04 **2** Look at the pictures. Listen to the story a

2

1

3

4

①

👧 今天的天气真舒服。

👧 明天你们做什么?

③

👧 我没时间,我要学唱歌和跳舞。

👦 我要学中国功夫。

ly.

第一题录音稿：

女孩：浩浩，你不舒服吗？

男孩：我生病了，头疼。

女孩：为什么？

男孩：我昨天很忙，太累了。昨天天气很热，所以我上午去游泳了。

女孩：下午呢？

男孩：我和姐姐一起唱歌和跳舞。

女孩：晚上呢？你几点休息？

男孩：我七点开始看功夫电影，九点打游戏，十二点休息。

我想在家上网打游戏。

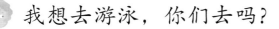
我想去游泳，你们去吗？

我昨天看了电影，明天想再去看。我们的活动真多！

第二题参考问题和答案：

How many activities are mentioned in the story? (There are 6 activities. Playing online games, swimming, singing and dancing, playing Chinese kung fu and watching a film.)

3 Complete the sentences. Write the letters and say.

a 生病　c 运动
b 再　　　d 功夫

1

我要运动，运动，再 _c_！

2

我 _a_ 了。

3

再见！我明年 _b_ 来！

4

中国 _d_ 真好玩。

Task

Michael Phelps 是美国游泳名将。他获得的奥运金牌数目是奥运历史之最。Taylor Swift 是美国著名的唱作歌手。Monkey King，孙悟空，是中国古典名著《西游记》中的主角之一。他擅长打斗，会多种法术。图中显示的是川剧《火焰山》。

Paste a photo of your favourite star or fictional character below.
Give a brief introduction and do a role-play.

他叫 Michael Phelps。
他游泳很快。

游泳、游泳、再游泳。

她叫 Taylor Swift。
她唱歌很好。

唱歌、唱歌、再唱歌。

他叫 Monkey King。
他功夫很好。

我跳、跳、再跳。

他/她叫 ……
他/她 ……

Paste your photo here.

……

Game

Play with your friend. Choose a word,
do the action and ask your friend
to say the word.

唱歌	跳舞	生病	上网
头疼	游泳	功夫	运动

跳舞。

Chant

Listen and say. 学生一边朗读儿歌一边做动作，加深
对儿歌中提到的各种活动的印象。

一二三，打功夫，
四五六，学游泳，
七八九，齐来做运动。

一二三，学唱歌，
四五六，来跳舞，
七八九，一起来活动。

放假了，时间多，
你运动，她歌舞，
时间用好身体好。

生活用语 Daily expressions

没时间了！

There is no time left!

我不太舒服。

I am not feeling very well.

写一写 Write

1 Trace and write the characters.

丶 丷 丗 呫 呫 唱 唱 唱 唱

唱 唱

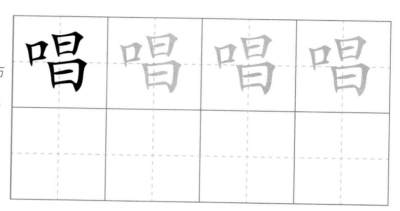

"唱"字右边是两个不同的字，上方的是"日"，比较瘦长，下方的是"曰"，比较宽扁，提醒学生切勿将两部分写成同样大小。

丨 刀 月 日 日 时 时
丶 亅 门 门 问 间 间

提醒学生注意"时"和"间"两个字里边的"日"写法的差别。相对来说，"时"字中的"日"更瘦长。

2 Trace 日 to complete the characters on the left. Then write and say.

早上   时间

日

太阳   唱歌

1 早上的太阳真好看。
2 今天我要学唱歌，没时间游泳。

16

提醒学生在填空之前先将段落和下方的选填字通读一遍。第一空和最后一空的答案是唯一的，所以可以先填好这两个空帮助段落理解。从第二空开始，每个空都有两个选项，需要结合上下文得出答案。

3 Complete the passage to help the ant find its way home. Draw the correct route.

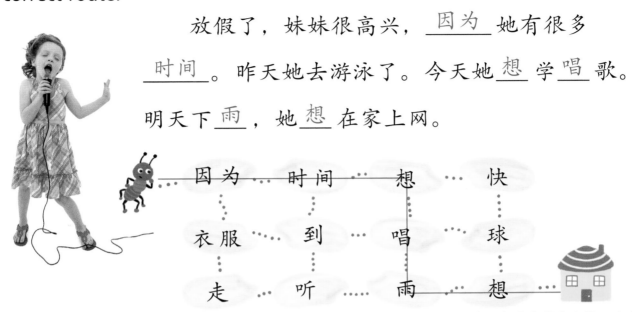

放假了，妹妹很高兴，<u>因为</u>她有很多 <u>时间</u>。昨天她去游泳了。今天她<u>想</u>学<u>唱</u>歌。明天下<u>雨</u>，她<u>想</u>在家上网。

因为	时间	想	快
衣服	到	唱	球
走	听	雨	想

中文和英文标点的使用有相似之处，但也有不少差异。例如，英文的句号是实心小点，但中文是空心的。中文还比英文多了顿号，在并列词语间，英文使用逗号，而中文使用顿号。在"说"字后面加直接引语时，中文是用冒号加双引号。

拼音输入法 Pinyin input

Chinese punctuation marks are different from the English ones. Pay special attention to their shapes and usage when typing Chinese sentences.

1 Tick the sentences with the correct punctuation marks and type them.

a ☑ 我星期一、星期二和星期六都不忙。

☐ 我星期一，星期二和星期六都不忙.

b ☐ 哥哥说，'我喜欢熊猫，它们太可爱了！'

☑ 哥哥说："我喜欢熊猫，它们太可爱了！"

2 Complete the sentences using the correct punctuation marks and type the sentences.

　、　，　。　？　！　：　"　"

姐姐说 : " 游泳真累 ！ 弟弟 ， 你饿了吗 ？

这里有饼干 、 三明治和鸡蛋 。 你想吃什么？ "

多元学习 Connections

中国功夫又叫中国武术，相传最早可以溯源至远古时代与野兽搏斗时的攻防技巧。中国功夫门派众多，比较出名的有太极拳和少林武术等。太极拳既可自卫也可健身，现已成为中国的全民体育活动。少林武术的每个套路都建立在中国古代的人体医学知识之上，合乎人体运动规律。

1 Have you watched any kung fu films? Do you know any of the kung fu schools? Learn about Chinese kung fu.

Chinese kung fu (martial arts) is a system of fighting. It has a long history in China.

我踢、踢、再踢！

慢慢打，别太快。

T'ai chi

There are various kung fu families, schools or sects across China.

我们跳、跳、再跳！

Shaolin martial arts

我爱中国功夫。

Practising Chinese kung fu helps strengthen one's body and mind.

2 Can you do these kung fu stances? Practise with your friend.

提醒学生做以上功夫动作时要量力而为，以免拉伤肌肉。

Project

京剧是中国的国剧，发源地在北京，最初因备受达官贵人的喜爱而逐渐流传。
2010年，京剧被列入人类非物质文化遗产代表作名录。

1 Have you heard of Beijing Opera? Read about it and find out the secret behind the colour scheme of its facial make-up (lianpu).

Beijing Opera is a Chinese form of opera which combines speech, singing, mime, acrobatics and music. The performers paint their faces different colours to represent different characteristics.

loyal, courageous

关羽，将领

upright, unyielding

尉迟恭，将领

brave, reckless

朱温，皇帝

fierce, ruthless

宇文成都，大将军，是小说中的虚拟人物

cunning

曹操，政治家、军事家

2 Design your own make-up pattern for any person or character. Show it to your friend and talk about it.

这是我的朋友/
Monkey King/……

他/她会……

他/她的脸是……色的，眼睛是……，鼻子是……

19

该对话是男孩和女孩在决定玩那个游戏前的一段对话，游戏分布在地图上不同的地方。角色扮演前，先让学生通读一遍对话，了解对话背景，再通过上下文和图片口头将空格补全并填写田字格。最后，学生两人一组，互相核对答案并进行角色扮演。

1 Complete the conversation and role-play with your friend.

游戏

开 始

Amy　Danny

1 下午有很多 _时间_。

时	间

2 我们上网玩游戏好吗？

3 太好了！开始吧。看，左边是我的照片，右边是你的 _照片_。

4 我们玩什么游戏？

5 我不想玩 _功夫_ 游戏和 _游泳_ 游戏。

6 我们再看看。我不太喜欢 _跳舞_ 游戏。

7 _唱歌_ 游戏怎么样？

唱	歌

8 好！

评核方法：
学生两人一组，互相考察评价表内单词和句子的听说读写。交际沟通部分由老师朗读要求，
学生再互相对话。如果达到了某项技能要求，则用色笔将星星或小辣椒涂色。

2 Work with your friend. Colour the stars and the chillies.

Words	说	读	写
时间	☆	☆	☆
功夫	☆	☆	🌶
唱歌	☆	☆	🌶
跳舞	☆	☆	🌶
上网	☆	☆	🌶
运动	☆	☆	🌶
再	☆	☆	🌶
照片	☆	🌶	🌶
游泳	☆	🌶	🌶
舒服	☆	🌶	🌶

Words and sentences	说	读	写
游戏	☆	🌶	🌶
生病	☆	🌶	🌶
疼	☆	🌶	🌶
我要运动、运动、再运动。	☆	🌶	🌶

Talk about leisure activities	☆

3 What does your teacher say?

评核建议：
根据学生课堂表现，分别给予"太棒了！
(Excellent!)"、"不错！(Good!)"或"继续努
力！(Work harder!)"的评价，再让学生圈出
上方对应的表情，以记录自己的学习情况。

My teacher says ...

分享 Sharing

Words I remember

时间	shí jiān	time
功夫	gōng fu	kung fu
唱歌	chàng gē	to sing
跳舞	tiào wǔ	to dance
上网	shàng wǎng	to go online
运动	yùn dòng	to do sports
再	zài	again, once more
照片	zhào piàn	photo
游泳	yóu yǒng	to swim
舒服	shū fu	well
游戏	yóu xì	game
生病	shēng bìng	to get sick
疼	téng	to ache

延伸活动：
1 学生用手遮盖英文，读中文单词，并思考单词意思；
2 学生用手遮盖中文单词，看着英文说出对应的中文单词；
3 学生两人一组，尽量运用中文单词分角色复述故事。

Other words

放假	fàng jià	to have a holiday
够	gòu	enough
用	yòng	to use
还	hái	also
拍	pāi	to take (a photo)
叫	jiào	to ask
天天	tiān tiān	every day
应该	yīng gāi	ought to, should
要	yào	to be determined

OXFORD
UNIVERSITY PRESS

Oxford University Press is a department of the University of Oxford.
It furthers the University's objective of excellence in research, scholarship,
and education by publishing worldwide. Oxford is a registered trade mark of
Oxford University Press in the UK and in certain other countries

Published in Hong Kong by
Oxford University Press (China) Limited
39th Floor, One Kowloon, 1 Wang Yuen Street, Kowloon Bay,
Hong Kong

© Oxford University Press (China) Limited 2017

The moral rights of the author have been asserted

First Edition published in 2017

Illustrated by Anne Lee, Emily Chan, KY Chan and Wildman

Photographs for reproduction permitted by Dreamstime.com

China National Publications Import & Export (Group) Corporation is an authorized distributor of
Oxford Elementary Chinese.

Please contact content@cnpiec.com.cn or 86-10-65856782

ISBN: 978-0-19-082257-6

10 9 8 7 6 5 4 3 2

Teacher's Edition
ISBN: 978-0-19-082269-9

10 9 8 7 6 5 4 3 2